THE
I HATE
NEW YORK
GUIDEBOOK

Warren D. Leight

with illustrations by Terry Allen

A Dell Trade Paperback

I dedicate this book to my landlord,
who, by failing to provide heat and hot water,
provided the inspiration for this book.

A DELL TRADE PAPERBACK

Published by
Dell Publishing Co., Inc.
1 Dag Hammarskjold Plaza
New York, New York 10017

Some of the material in this book first appeared, in a different
form, in *The Village Voice*.

ISBN: 0-440-53609-X

Printed in the United States of America

Designed by Richard Oriolo

Second printing—July 1983

Acknowledgments

The following people helped me with this book even though they all had more important things they should have been doing:

Don Perman, Edward Leight, Charles Kaufman, Cassandra Danz, Mary Fulham, Don and Timmy Leight, Rob Brill, Tracy Cochran, Jennifer Allen, Lori Andiman, and Bill Dyckes.

I'm also grateful for the support, insight, and intimidation provided by my editor, Gary Luke, and my agent, Rich Pine.

Finally, my deepest gratitude to Laurie Galen, to whom this book would have been dedicated had I not decided to go for the cheap joke that appears on the preceding page.

CONTENTS

Introduction   1

How to Get Around New York   3

How to Spend in New York   18

Where and How to Dine in New York   32

Neighborhoods   50

If You Must Live in New York   65

The Manhattan SAT   81

INTRODUCTION

Admit it.

You don't really love New York. You never have, and you never will.

You've been living a lie.

Don't be ashamed, you're not alone. The truth is, no one loves New York. The truth is . . .

You hate New York. Say it. Go on, say it:

I HATE NEW YORK.

Say it.

There. You feel a lot better now. A weight has been lifted. Think of fresh air and clean streets. Affordable homes. Service with a smile. Well-paved roads. Children playing. Wildflowers. Think of your high school prom. Shag rugs.

Think of your mother.

The truth is that with the possible exception of your mother, New York has none of these things. New York instead has a reverse Midas touch.

Do any of these sentiments sound familiar?

> You hate your landlord.
> You hate waiting in line for three hours to see a bad movie in a cramped, overpriced theater.
> You hate singles' bars, Laundromats, and the phone company.
> You hate waiting an hour for a bus and then watching six of them arrive as if they were a convoy.
> You hate the Yankees; you hate the Mets.

Do you feel as if you could add to this list?

Go ahead! Get it out of your system!

What you are feeling is good and honest. What you are feeling is normal. Don't bottle up your rage. Go with it. You are not alone. Millions of people, all over the world, hate New York. Millions of people all over New York hate New York.

HOW TO GET AROUND NEW YORK

It's so simple to get around New York. The entire city is laid out on a grid (see map). Note that:

—Even-numbered streets run east; odd numbered run west.

—Most avenues are numbered and run either north or south.

—Lettered avenues run through bad neighborhoods.

—Purse snatchers run through traffic yelling "Stop, thief!" and point ahead of themselves.

—Broadway snakes the length of the city's grid like a Gila monster on acid.

How Can I Get Around New York?

There are five basic modes of travel in New York: subway, bus, taxi, car, and stolen car. Each mode carries its own stress. In general, for every hour spent trying to go cross-town in mid-Manhattan, subtract a week from your life span.

If you travel this route by subway late at night, subtract your life span from your life span.

Are Subways for Me?

Subways are for the young, the carefree, the dynamic. Subways are for people in a hurry who also have nothing to live for. If you can hold your breath for hours, and don't mind strangers grinding your sacroiliac into dust, subways may be for you.

Are Subways Clean?

Heh.

Every morning the entire city subway system is hosed down with a urine-scented disinfectant. Long, winding pedestrian tunnels are given a special double coating.

How Do I Understand My Motorman?

New York is a melting pot; people from all over the world ride the city's subways. Rest assured that the men guiding your train have taken special motorman speech courses. Train stops and transit updates are announced in Universal Subway Code:

ANNOUNCEMENT	TRANSLATION
Tisk quid op suan	Times Square
We'll be experiencing a short delay	Kiss your job good-bye
Lesefrak eyonek screw	Change here for the Number Two train
This is a local train making express stops only ubenhaz furtig street then brishgii	You may never see your family again
Lesefrak eyonek poltergeist	Change here for the BMT line
Please move away from the closing doors, there's another train right behind this one	Your check is in the mail

What Would Happen If the Russians Were to Invade and Occupy New York?

Above ground, traffic hasn't moved in decades. Transit planners fear the enemy would likely take over the subways in order to position troops, supplies, and borscht.

The system has been designed to thwart such a catastrophe:

—For years, savvy transit employees have posted erroneous, misleading signs and maps throughout the system. Recently many signs, and all maps, have been spray-painted over with graffiti as an added precaution.

—Each train is known by six or seven different names: The IRT = the Number One train = the Broadway local = the Seventh Avenue line = the South Ferry train.

—To further confuse those totalitarian bastards, each car of every train is marked with inaccurate and conflicting destination signs. If it says "South Ferry," you can bet the train is going north.

SUBWAY SAFETY TIPS

1) Never, ever establish eye contact with anyone over three years of age. Babies are technically okay, but follow your instincts.

2) Bring reading material so you don't absently catch the eyes of a staring psychopath. Do **not** read the **New York Post**—it seems to attract the very people you're trying to avoid.

3) Assume that anyone who rubs or touches any part of your body or briefcase is a sexual deviant who couldn't even get into the army. If a pervert persists in "copping a feel," shout at the top of your lungs: "You paid **seventy-five** cents to ride the subway, not my ass!" When you shout on the subway, everyone, including perverts, edges away.

4) Do not play social worker. The subway is the world's largest outpatient clinic. There is at least one psycho/sexual maladjust for every car in the system.

5) Do what the crowd does:
   a) If everyone on a train laughs at the crazy man, laugh along.
   b) If everyone ignores him, you must ignore him, too! This is hard to do at first. You are just not used to the sounds of a bile-filled man screaming, "Rockefeller makes a million dollars a minute, Rockefeller makes a million dollars a minute." Practice ignoring friends and family. Remember, if everyone pretends the raving lunatic isn't there, he isn't there.
   c) If everyone panics, you panic, too. When you sense hysteria building, take the lead. Scream, push, and bribe your way into the next car. Close the door behind you.

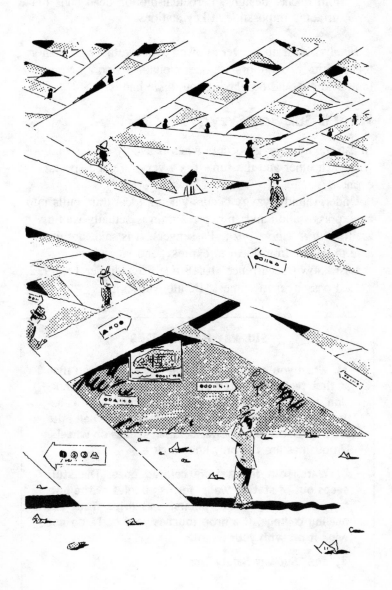

—Staircases, ramps, and escalators were all constructed from Escher designs. Perpetual-motion dead ends make surfacing impossible at key stations.

Finally, no train is ever allowed to leave the yard if more than a third of its doors are operational—a smooth commuter flow would be playing into *their* hands.

What Is Subway Syzygy?

In astronomy, syzygy occurs when heavenly bodies line up with each other and the sun. It is a very rare and special event.

Underground, syzygy occurs when a local train pulls into an express station and an express train is actually waiting for it, *with its doors open*. Passengers, it is said, are then able to *switch* from local to express, and vice versa.

Last known occurrence: 10:18 P.M., September 14, 1932. Last passenger to witness: Benito Mussolini.

SUBWAY HEALTH TIPS

1) When you emerge from the Black Hole, you may at first feel disoriented and out of sorts. The condition, known as BMT-lag, can strike anytime. It is especially common in summer months when the subways become poltergeist-ridden saunas on wheels. Limousines are the only known cure.

2) Watch out for weirdly colored ooze. The stuff seeps out of station walls, forms puddles at the bottom of subway girder pillars, and drips from the peeling ceilings. If a drop touches your body, do **not** wipe it off with your hand!

3) See "Subway Safety Tips."

Zen and the Art of Bus Riding

Buses require Eastern patience. Rid yourself of Western self-ishness and anxiety.

Believe that the bus you are waiting for will come, if not in this lifetime, then the next.

You are ready to ride a bus if you understand that the journey may be a long one; that knowing your destination does not mean you have found your path. Understand that the journey may never end, and this, too, is part of life's cycle.

Accept all forms of life on the bus as your brother.

Accept that there is no way to look out of a bus. Look inside your soul rather than out the spray-painted, soot-basted windows.

Time to Meditate

As your bus crawls through the city's gnarled avenues, you will have time to meditate on the basic questions of Zen Bus Mastery:

—If a bus is air conditioned, but no one has ever felt the air conditioning, is the bus really air conditioned at all?

—What is goo, and why are the seats and floors covered with it?

—Is the man in the back of this bus too crazy to sit next to?

If the bus should be crowded, ask:

—Of the people rubbing my body, how many are rubbing it accidentally; how many on purpose? How many parts of my body are being rubbed?

—Why do the big guys seated in the back of the bus keep their legs spread so wide apart?

—Is that a shopping bag between my legs?

If the bus should be crowded during off-peak hours, ask:
    —How many of the people on this bus have a job?
    How many of the people on this bus can *spell job*?

To be a Zen Master at peace, you must also learn the two questions not to ask, for they will trouble your spirit:
    —Why do buses, like birds of paradise, shun the night and the rain?
    —Why do buses, like rabid dogs, come only in packs of ten, spaced hours apart?

Remember, finally, the *way* is available only to those with exact change.

RIGHT   WRONG

Cabbies—That Old Hack Magic

The New York cabbie is gone. That old smart-alecky driver who knew every corner of the city has gone the way of the nickel ferry, the cheap garret in Greenwich Village, the gang wars fought only with switchblades. In thirty years the hack has undergone a transition from Cabbie-as-Philosopher to Cabbie-as-Bore to today's dominant Cabbie-as-Psychopath.

PHILOSOPHER   BORE   PSYCHO

Language

Philosopher: Brooklynese; English with a Flatbush lilt:
"So dis guy goes, 'If youse two don't stop . . .' "

Bore: Jaded, despair-filled clichés; modeled on Hollywood version of philosopher cabbie, only with nothing to say:
"It's not what you know, but who you know."
"This city was paradise before that goddamn Lindsay."

Psycho: Believed to speak a dialect that combines Sumerian, Classical Profane, and several other dead languages from the Hamito-Semitic family; his English consists of only a few rants:
"I no can break ten-dollar bill."
"Dees city crazy, crazy dees city."

Hobbies and Interests

Philosopher: Six newspapers a day; all-news radio. Chess. Baseball. Dialectics, family, block association. Sunday-morning interview shows.

Bore: Nostalgia radio. TV, especially *All in the Family* reruns where Archie sticks it to the meathead son-in-law. Enjoys looking at pictures of self in aging, gravy-and-sauce-stained high school yearbook.

Psycho: Drives cab. In spare time drives cab for cousin. Goes to strange belly-dancing disco clubs in West Thirties.

Eating Habits

Philosopher: Wife's cooking in brown bag. Cafeteria: pastrami on rye. Borscht. Salami and sour cream.

Bore: Street vendors at red lights: hot dog with everything on it. If no vendors around, he scrapes sauerkraut off T-shirt.

Psycho: Coffee with twelve sugars, Benzedrine, Methedrine, Oreos. Maraschino cherry juice and syrup.

Favorite Discussion Topics

Philosopher: The inherent contradictions of being a wage earner, and a patriot, in a society dominated by an insulated economic elite. Augie Donatelli, Donatello, Sandy Koufax. The limited prospects for the Brooklyn Dodgers/New York Mets and socialism.

Bore: "Goddamn Mayor Lindsay giving the city away to welfare chiselers while my driveway in Queens is covered with snow; you know whad I'm talkin' about? Right?"

Psycho: (Delivered while strangling the steering wheel) "My wife, I loved her. God, how I loved her. But she go crazy. Crazy in head. Seven years she see doctor. Then we marry she goes buy thirty thousand dollar furniture for house. Thirty thousand dollar. I say, 'You no see doctor, I have to pay furniture.' She go really crazy like nothing. Gets lawyer says I no can go near her. My wife. Now I drive eighteen hours a day to pay alimony, to furniture pay, cab. I kill her if I see her. God, how I loved her.''

Appearance

Philosopher: Cap, open-collar check shirt from Alexander's. Beard, optional cigar. Sunburned left elbow; a few liver spots.
Bore: Overweight, needs shave. No longer uses toothbrush. Sauce-and-gravy-stained T-shirt. Perpetual glower, actively depressed.
Psycho: Makes Travis "You Talkin' to Me?" Bickel look like Phil Donahue. One set of Third-World-Hip polyester clothes. Shirt open revealing hairy chest, and medallion that seems to represent the Slaughter of the Innocents.

What About Keeping a Car in New York?

New York is the only city in the world where having a car subtracts from your mobility. City roads are pockmarked like the face of a mass murderer. Pedestrians taunt you, cabbies torture you, pigeons stare you down.

New cars rust before your eyes.

Is There Plenty of Free Parking?

In the time it takes to find a parking place, you could locate the Ark of the Covenant.

Once parked, you need only worry about your car getting ticketed, towed away, vandalized, burglarized, or sodomized.

Is It Safe to Park on the Streets?

When you park your car in New York, you are essentially leaving a mobile ten-thousand-dollar bill on the sidewalk. There is very little reason for it to be there the next day.

Should your car survive a New York night of the living dead, it's a sure bet that all removable contents—tape player, suitcases, backseat—will be gone.

Why Are All Those People in Nightgowns Double-Parking Their Cars?

Every morning in New York, at exactly eight A.M., thousands of sleepwalkers, clad only in slippers and robes, emerge from deep REM to move their cars to the other, *alternate,* side of the street. They double-park, blocking those cars that didn't have to move, and then they go back to sleep.

Three hours later they move their cars back.

This bizarre ritual is theoretically intended to facilitate street cleaning. Sadly, *no street has ever been cleaned during this interval.* Instead, squadrons of meter maids use this time to blitzkrieg whole boroughs.

How Thorough Are the Meter Maids?

If all city services were performed with half the efficiency of ticketing, New York would make Zurich look like Tijuana.

How About Garaging My Vehicle?

If you absolutely cannot find a parking space, you might think of saving up enough to put the car in a parking lot or garage. In midtown Manhattan the hourly rate for parking is pegged to the hourly rate of a top-drawer corporate tax law-yer plus the city's fourteen percent garage sales tax.

Note: If you are checked into a hotel, expect the under-ground parking fee to exceed the room fee. Also expect the garage to be cleaner and brighter than your room.

Garages to Avoid:

Park and Pray
Lock and Lose
Park and Prey

Traveler's Advisory

Arrival in New York

If you are arriving by plane and have a lot to carry, you might consider taking a taxi to the city. From La Guardia Airport to midtown should run around twenty bucks. If you are an illiterate Iraqi exchange student, figure on spending about $457. There's no need to tell your driver that you are from out of town. He will know.

If you are driving into New York, a special treat is in store for you at the first long red light: Bowery bums have been franchised to all bridge and tunnel exits. There they eke out a spare-change existence by surrounding your car and threatening to wash your windshield with a filthy rag or used bandage. You can pay a fast fifty cents, or, when the light changes, see how many winos can fit on the head of your windshield.

You pay a toll only as you enter New York. No one leaving New York has that kind of money.

Transportation Quiz

Before you grapple with New York's immensely complicated transportation reticulum, you might want to take:
   a) Several Valium.
   b) This quiz.

Which of these people would you be surprised to see on a city bus?
   a) Blond, blue-eyed, blue-blazered prep schoolers fearful of D train disembowelment.
   b) Wimps.
   c) Princess Di.
   d) Godot.

Answer True/False:
   —The Transit Authority raided the Weimar Republic for financial planners.
   —Evel Knievel said he would not drive a Chevy Nova across the Fifty-ninth Street Bridge.
   —The city's bridges and roadways all date from the hunting-and-gathering stage of the Pleistocene epoch.
   —Cabbies in Bangkok speak more English than cabbies in New York.

ESSAY: Many scientists believe that the problem of nuclear waste disposal would be solved if the stuff were left inside a locked car overnight in New York. Do you agree?

HOW TO
SPEND IN NEW YORK

The city is a cash-sucking vortex; a scavenger metropolis. The year's savings of a vacationer can disappear in one evening—in one ride from the airport, if the vacationer doesn't speak English.

Money vanishes here so quickly, so often, you'll need twenty-four-hour access to it.

How to Get Money

Cashing Personal Checks: There is no one in New York who will cash your check. Not even your mother. It is unheard of for a store to accept a local check—how do you think they'll feel about one drawn from Muncie?

Cashing Traveler's Checks: Best to leave home without them. Even internationally welcomed checks get the cold shoulder in this trustless town. What may be cashable in Kabul is considered bogus on Broadway.

Banks *may* cash them if a local friend puts his savings account down as collateral.

Never ask in advance if a restaurant or cabbie will take your traveler's check. Eat the meal first, then offer the check as your only form of payment.

Cashing Cash: Not as easy as you might imagine. New York constantly demands payment in small, unmarked bills.

If you have big bills, try to break them before your arrival. A five or over will incur your news dealer's wrath. A

CASHING CASH: BASIC DIALOGUE

Note: If you must break a big bill (a five or over), try to establish cashier eye-contact before you begin. Beg forgiveness and smile like a serf.

Cashier
(while blowing gum bubble)
Don't you got anything smaller?

You
I'm sorry, it's all I have.

Cashier
I don't got no change. What do you think this is, a bank or somethin'?

You
(looking down at linoleum)
I'm terribly sorry. I just came from the cash machine, they don't give singles. I'm really sorry. Here, let me buy some gum, too.

(At this point, cashier will examine your bill for signs of counterfeiting. You begin to sweat. The manager will now be called in to "approve" your twenty; he's always called Frankie):

Cashier
Frankie! . . . Frankie! Check twenty! Yo, Frankie!

Frankie
(After suitable wait he stops talking on phone, examines your bill.)
Don't you got anything smaller?

(If you've held out this long, and if a disgruntled line is forming behind you, Frankie will cave in. Muttering dark religious curses under his nicotine breath, he will do you this favor this one time. He will allow you to buy something from his store.)

twenty might drive the guy in the deli to come at you with a carving knife.

Cash Machine: The bank cash machine has become a lifeline, providing enough of a fix to get you through lunch, through dinner, through last call. At four A.M. the New Yorker is not surprised to find himself waiting ten-people deep on a cash-machine line, each paranoiac desperate for one last infusion to get home safely—"Better a cabbie should take all your money than a mugger."

How to Keep a Budget in New York

1) New York on Five Dollars a Day:
   Drop dead.
2) New York on Ten Dollars a Day:
   Eat breakfast, then drop dead.

I Hate New York Budget Tips

1) Leave the house or hotel with no money and no way of getting any. This is *very* important, because no matter how much cash you start with, by the end of the day you'll have no money left, and nothing to show for it.

2) Carry only out-of-state checks. It's easier to pass a kidney stone.

3) Hoard small change. You need exact change for change machines here. Storekeepers are petty extortionists who force you to buy gum or a paper in order to get change for the bus. Resist buying something in Bloomingdale's just to get a dime for the pay phone.

4) Ignore panhandlers. They want your spare change (see Rule 3). Even Sister Teresa pinches quarters when she blows into New York.

Where to Shop in New York

New York is a shopper's paradise! A twenty-five-hour city; zestful, dynamic, glowing!

Where else but in New York can you buy a toaster oven at four thirty in the morning? A genuine Rolex watch for fourteen bucks? A late-model Cadillac for three thousand dollars—cash only—?

Where but in New York, crazy, teeming city of trade. And where but in New York can you buy your own recently pilfered stereo, at a deep discount, from the back of a van parked in midtown?

New York is a markdown mecca. Go explore, and remember, being strip-searched by a security guard on the way out is half the fun!

Fifth Avenue

This is of course the holiest of holy grounds for shoppers. Devoted buyers and career consumers pilgrimage here from all over the world to bathe in the perfumed vapors of the first-floor cosmetics sections.

In a powerful rite of passage, gold-and-pearl-laden mothers bring their pigtailed daughters to Bonwit Teller and take them through a series of divine rituals, culminating in the

"I COULDN'T B'LEEVE IT, THEN HE GOEZ..."

Estée Lauder Personal Makeover. "Today I am a woman. Today I learned to charge."

In Lower East Side bargain basements, it is whispered that "God invented these people because someone had to pay retail."

There are two kinds of stores on Fifth Avenue: high-maintenance stores for the high bourgeoisie, and high fraud for the highly naive (see chart).

Bloomingdale's

Bloomie's used to cater to aristocracy but in recent years has shifted to duping the hoi polloi and upwardly mobile. Shoppers are mesmerized by gold chrome, black marble, and mirrors—the look and feel of an Egyptian sarcophagus. Merchandising and libido, always intertwined, become one here. Charge-account customers experience afterglow. Bloomie's is perhaps best known for its pioneer Cult of Cultural Consumption. Once a year Bloomie's:

1) Combs the globe in search of a new, impoverished Third World country;
2) Buys out the foreign culture—Bloomie's buyers travel cash in hand;
3) Returns to New York; arranges a film festival, an embassy fashion show, and a stunning window display.

Whoosh! The whole city's suddenly gone Senegalese, or batty for Belize, or crazy for Kuala Lumpur.

Though you are paying top dollar for that Sri Lanka sweater, barely a penny of it is trickling back to the native village craftsmen. Bloomingdale's would not want to disrupt a centuries-old way of life.

As in all major department stores, there is no longer a staff available to assist you. Cashiers are scattered near escalators; their motto is Service with a sneer.

Two Types of Fifth Avenue Shops

	HIGH MAINTENANCE	*HIGH FRAUD*
TYPICAL NAMES	Bonwit Teller, Bergdorf Goodman, Gucci, Fortunoff, Saks Fifth Avenue	Farouk's, Farid's Persia Palace, Ishmael Video
AMBIENCE AND DESIGN	Quiet, calm, insulated. An enclave secluded from the harsh world—like a Sheraton Hotel in Marrakesh. Image is everything, darling: wood display cases, crystal chandeliers, pastel-colored Doric columns—the Hapsburgs could mistake it for home.	A Naples black market. Huge LIQUIDATION and GOING OUT OF BUSINESS posters, all covered with dust. Fluorescent lights and sagging pressboard shelves. Shag rug bought used from VD clinic; littered with cigarette butts, held together with masking tape at heavy traffic junctures.
LAYOUT AND PRODUCTS	Orderly, very orderly. Porcelain gives way to flatware, gives way to silver. Watches are called timepieces; candy is sold by a "chocolatier." First floor redolent with hundred-dollar-a-dram perfume; eighty-five percent of the world's known rouge reserves.	Silk-and-wool handmade Persian rugs next to Kitchen Kritter oven mitts next to Nairobi zebra skins next to fake Samsonite luggage next to porno video cassettes next to embroidered tablecloths next to Onega watches

SALES STAFF   Blue-hairs. Young, well-dressed impoverished underachievers, angry at the world. Male staff closely resemble palace eunuchs.

Chain-smoking swarthy guys in sweat-stained poly shirts. Neck open to reveal chest hair and gold religious medallions.

SERVICE   Basically trained to ignore you. Older women pepper speech with "Listen, dearie" and "Sorry, honey." Unless you're a regular, they'll let you choke to death on the floor.

When a tourist enters, six guys immediately drop their backgammon games and accost him: "My friend, my friend, we sell here only dee best. Ninety dollars wholesale, I give to you sixty-three dollars, no tax." Can curse and fleece in nine languages.

PRICES   High quality, higher prices. A child's confirmation dress checks in at about the price of a Datsun. Payment accepted in *old money*: pre-1936 silver certificates, French sous. Charge available, but applications are inherited.

Name brands at four to five times list price; unfortunately all name-brand items are fake. They'll take the shirt off your back, sew a designer label on it, and sell it back to you at a price that covers their Fifth Avenue rent. Accept all currency: shekels, yen, guineas, Confederate railroad bonds, even lire—their exchange rates apply.

UPTOWN   DOWNTOWN

SoHo

How to Shop in SoHo—World Famous Gallery District
1) Buy a parachute;
2) Tie it around your waist;
3) Promenade down West Broadway; take care to avoid all galleries!
4) Buy white wine in exposed brick café; discuss galleries.

5) If you have a trust fund
  a) enter boutique;
  b) try to distinguish mannequins from clerks;
  c) buy a fourteen-hundred-dollar Mylar parachute sweater for your next trip to SoHo.

5) If you don't have a trust fund
  a) go to Prince Street postcard store;
  b) browse for half an hour;
  c) go home.

The Whoopee Cushion District (Broadway, Eighteenth to Twenty-third streets)

What is it about New York that breeds such creativity? The cutting edge in novelty-item design for the free world.

The Nehru Jacket District (Broadway, Fifteenth to Eighteenth streets)

Also stocks hard-to-find bell-bottoms and love beads.

Grotesque Neo-Baroque Italian Furniture District (Grand Street off Bowery)

They say Rocky shopped here after he made it. Rococo on parade.

Used Industrial Kitchen Supply District (Bowery, south of Houston)

Great buys on two-tier, eight-pie Bari pizza ovens and never-need-cleaning eight-gallon coffee makers.

Chop Shop District (Bay Ridge, Brooklyn)

Mile after mile of stores selling stolen auto parts. Trained mechanics can instantly turn any make of car into several hundred discounted spare parts. Drive on down; be sure to lock your doors.

Tombstone and Monument Showplace (E. Houston Street)

Good place for discounts on items ordered but never picked up.

The Lower East Side (Houston to Canal, east of the Bowery)

Every Sunday, oversize baby-blue Chevrolets from the sub-urbs ferry in thousands of linen-craving princesses who will trample you to death in their quest for name-brand mark-downs. Storekeepers are angry and paranoiac. They keep luggage in chains, hosiery behind wire cages, stacks of de-

signer jeans under thick, taut rope. They wish it were
barbed wire. Try not to get talked into buying twelve pairs
of knee socks at ''wholesale.''

SHOPPING FOR BARGAINS ON THE LOWER EAST SIDE
BASIC DIALOGUE

Shopper Number One
Excuse me, where's your dressing room?

Storekeeper
(cursing his lot in life)
The pants are fifteen dollars, and she expects to get
a dressing room, too.

Shopper Number One
I just want to make sure they fit.

Storekeeper
I'm thirty years in the business and she wants to
know if it will fit her. Like a glove it will fit.

Shopper Number One
But I'm thin-waisted.

Storekeeper
So you take it in a little. Fifteen dollars you can't go
wrong. The bastards uptown in the big stores want
twenty-five, same pair. . . . I'm running a nonprofit
organization.

Seasoned Shopper Number Two
Excuse me. . . . I'm not standing here for my health!

Storekeeper (to Shopper Number Two)
Lady, God forbid you should wait your turn, like this
nice lady did. (to SHOPPER NUMBER ONE) Lady, you're
ruining my business. Buy the pants. There's a tailor
around the corner, second floor. Tell him I sent you
to try on the pants. If they don't fit, bring them back.
. . . A charity I'm running here.

Union Square Park—Scoring "Al Fresco". . . . or Else!

There are literally scores of parks, miniparks, and just plain ol' street corners where drugs are retailed to the public. One has only to go to the corporate plazas of Wall Street or midtown at noon to "cop" some "loose joints 'n' bags, my man, joints 'n' bags."

So what is it about Union Square that makes buying drugs here so . . . quintessentially New York? Sure, there are more dealers than most places; sure, they'll sell you anything—black beauties, *tres* bags, the stuff that killed Bruce Lee—but there's more to it than that. It has to do with the fiery qualities of the salesmen themselves. In a word: real New Yorkers.

These fellas are like the saucy old deli men of bygone days. We went to the park one day and within seconds of sitting down on a bench, we were approached by several men, all dressed to kill. "You here to cop?" they asked us.

Though they undoubtedly had top-notch, pure drugs (indeed they said as much), we just weren't in the mood.

"No, thanks, just here to pass a little time."

"Look," came the reply, "if you're not here to cop drugs, get out of our park. Now."

We left, of course.

Remember, it's a lovely park, but, in order to meet expenses, there *is* a nickel-bag minimum.

How to Understand Your Local Merchant

Store Purchases

WHEN THEY SAY:	THEY MEAN:
May I help you?	Buy or get out!
It's slightly irregular.	This jacket has three sleeves.

For you, fifteen dollars.	I see you're a tourist.
Don't let my boss know I sold it to you for this price.	I see you were born yesterday.
Check your bag, lady?	I'd like to cut your hands off at the wrist.
I can give it to you without the box.	This is a floor model that has been abused by eight hundred crazed shoppers.
Money cheerfully refunded.	You must be high.

Street Purchases

Dime.	Ten dollars; thus, dime bag means a ten-dollar bag, or packet, of marijuana. Similarly nickel bag.
Yard.	One hundred dollars. Synonyms: bill and C-note.
K.	One thousand (from kilo). Also, more generally to indicate good sums of money, as in "My man is earning some K now!"
Chump change.	Sums of money so small as to be worthless. Not worth bending down to pick up. In New York, anything under a yard.
Check it out, check it out.	Come, examine my wares.
Yo, my man.	Pardon me, sir, if I might have your attention for just a few moments.
I got the gold, got the gold.	I have available for purchase high-grade Colombian and Acapulco marijuana.

Games New Yorkers Play

Furniture-Hunting Safari

By the time New Yorkers have paid their rents they have no money left to furnish their apartments.

Instead, they scour the streets, rifling through uncollected garbage. (Note: *uncollected garbage* is a redundant term in New York.) They'll recycle the most pitiful throwaways. On the West Side, and downtown, it's the Berkeley look: milk crates, cement blocks, roach-infested Formica shards.

On the Upper East Side the furniture-hunting New Yorker finds himself in Naugahyde Nirvana, Haitian cotton heaven. These side streets boast discarded furniture that is better than the furniture found inside most other New York apartments. Sadly, this furniture will not fit inside most other New York apartments. To play, bring a chainsaw with you and take home the better half of a fine Chippendale highboy. (Note: this is one of the few New York neighborhoods where a lone man with a chainsaw will look conspicuous on the street.) Try not to point it at the little girls in knee socks and plaid skirts. (Oh, go ahead, point it.)

WHERE AND HOW TO DINE IN NEW YORK

If your bathtub were in your kitchen, would you want to eat at home?

No matter how much you like to cook, no matter how good a cook you are, when you come to New York, you end up eating out. All the time. Harassed and oppressed at work, at home, and in between, the New Yorker seeks refuge in restaurants.

You and Your Waiter

The New York waiter is a legend. While the menu may coyly say "Our pleasure to serve you," the New York waiter derives his pleasure from demeaning you. He "cops an attitude."

His object is to make you sorry you ever walked into his miserable chintzy eatery. To make you regret the whole lopsided power structure that allows pathetic, know-nothing curs like yourself to order service from others.

The waiter's task is a large one: he must destroy your day in as little time as possible because his manager wants turnover. He is assisted by busboys who are paid by the decibel.

How to Get Water in a Restaurant

This is, of course, against the law in New York. If you should ask for water, most waiters will just nod in a nostalgic gesture.

If you *must* have water, pantomime the advanced stages of dehydration. When this fails, set fire to your neighbors' table.

Separate Checks
A phrase so obscene, so revolting, that no one dares utter it in public. To ask is to open yourself up to a galaxy of abuse.

Free Second Cup of Coffee
See "Separate Checks."

How to Tip

Violent Service—waiter threw knives, spilled boiling soup in your lap: fifteen percent.
Neutral Service—waiter disavowed knowledge of your existence: twenty percent.
Outstanding Service—waiter brought you some things: thirty percent.

How to Eat Breakfast

A New Yorker does not wake up at the crack of dawn, leap out of bed, and yell, "This is the first day of the rest of my life!"

During the night he has been pummeled by traffic noise: police sirens, garbage trucks at four A.M., mobile teen-agers with big radios turned up real loud, inexplicable explosions.

The New Yorker awakens to another day of powerlessness. The only mystery is, How many indignities per hour will he suffer? How many dinner roaches still patrol his kitchen?

The New Yorker, or the visitor to New York, cannot *deal with* making breakfast. The entire population of the Greater Metropolitan Area head to coffee shops.

Here's how to separate the whole wheat from the shaft:

Where Not to Eat Breakfast

Hotel breakfast specials go beyond greed. Innkeepers know a drowsy, somnambulant tourist can't focus on menu prices. Enter the eleven-dollar scrambled egg—toast and coffee extra.

Some cognoscenti maintain that these overpriced breakfasts are the city's "power meals." Yes, New York's real movers and shakers take limos to break baguettes in the Ambassador Room at the United Nations Plaza Hotel.

Let them.

Just around the corner, drop a notch in pretentiousness and watch the bill drop by seventeen hundred percent. As any cabbie will tell you, "Eggs is eggs."

Where to Eat Breakfast

Every neighborhood has at least one genuine Greek-American coffee shop. There the breakfast specials have names like "Plow Boy" or "Farmer Boy."

No one in New York knows what these terms mean; locals bypass the quaint names and just submit their orders.

The smart money goes for two eggs ("any style"), toast, home fries, coffee, and orange juice for a buck and a half. The toast comes too dry or too greasy; put in a special request for whole wheat or rye lest they slip you white bread. The home fries have been aged on the grill for at least six weeks. Orange juice is served in the smallest glass size visible to the naked eye.

When to Eat Breakfast

Time your arrival with care. One minute after the special ends, the price is liable to double on the same order. The earlier the breakfast special ends, the more up-scale and up-tight the neighborhood:

> **Upper East Side:** rich getting richer. Testosterone-loaded, fast-tracking professionals. Prices are higher. Croissants have replaced toast. People speed-read *The Wall Street Journal* while chewing eggs. Special ends as early as nine A.M.

Upper West Side: musicians hotbedding cramped apartments, actors on unemployment, writers, sociologists, academics. Single adult males alone in booths reading every word of every section of *The New York Times*. Special goes to eleven A.M.

East Village: aging socialists, would-be New Wave rock stars dressed in black. Phone-company workers, civil servants on extended breaks, foreign artists in search of Hopper's America. The breakfast special goes until three P.M., weekends until five P.M.

A SHORT HISTORY AND GUIDE TO GREEK-AMERICAN COFFEE SHOPS

Shortly after the Opium Wars, New York was carved up into several foreign concessions. Indians and Pakistanis got the newsstands, Koreans got the fruit stands, and Greeks were handed every coffee shop in the Greater Metropolitan Area.

Shortly thereafter every coffee shop, using a modular design approach, was turned into a holy temple of visual alienation. Each shop is named after a latent-homosexual Greek god. Each shop features the same menu and each shop boasts the same thirty-three artificial surfaces, including:

- Photos of Butcher Block laminated over Illusion-o'-Wood Tables.
- Fake fieldstone walls.
- Fake Old West wooden chandeliers lit by bulbs in the shape of candle flames, "burning" on plastic in the shape of candles.
- Fake dollar bill over the cash register.
- Imitation-of-Leatherette seat covering.
- Styrofoam pastry wrapped in plastic (no need to unwrap before eating).

The Truth About Coffee to Go

Los Angeles runs on gas, Chicago runs on steel. New York runs on caffeine. In midtown and Wall Street it's set-up-the-caffeine-IV . . . to go. To travel. To take out.

"Lemme getta container of coffee, light."
"Coffee, sweet and light."

No one sits down for coffee in a midtown shop; these places too closely resemble housing-project elevators.

No one knows what "coffee regular" means—especially the counterman.

New York coffee demands starch: a bagel, a kaiser roll with butter, a Danish (plastic-wrapped and mass produced—prune, cheese, or plain), a modular bran muffin "high and dry" (toasted, no butter).

Gotham Java can't be swallowed black. The urns haven't been cleaned since Dewey won.

New York coffee containers, to go, always have a picture of the Parthenon on the sides.

The Parthenon has a picture of a New York coffee container on its sides.

Metropolitan mocha comes with plastic lids that do not really fit but don't start to leak until you've left the store.

New York cops buy more coffees-to-go than all of Europe, Boston, Philadelphia, and the entire Third World.

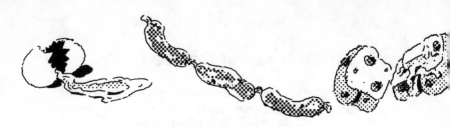

Lunches: Fact or Fiction

New York lunches. The very term conjures up images of pinstripes and power. Rows of limousines double-parked outside Lutèce, Four Seasons, "21."

Inside, the same gray guys who had power breakfasts four hours ago are at it again, lounging over the "deal lunch." Vodka-tonic appetizers, thick rare steaks. For the vegetarians, there's steak with onions.

If you're visiting New York, you know that's what you want.

Forget it. They'll never seat you. You'll have to fight it out with four million wage earners who have a little over an hour to handle all their shopping and banking, and they must also order food, be served, eat, overtip, and pay.

You'll learn what New York lunchtime really means.

Lunch is eaten standing up at a ten-inch counter that faces an iron-poor wall.

Lunch in New York pits behind-the-counter expertise against deeply ingrained anarchy. Anarchy wins. Fast-food chains, known the world over for consistent if mediocre quality, fail miserably in this hyped-up harbor town.

Instead of being hospital-clean, they're knee-deep in trash; the garbage cans look like Vesuvius ready to blow.

Instead of hot fries and cold cakes, all food is served at room temperature; the only thing fried is the staff.

Instead of a wholesome bring-the-family atmosphere, it's a war zone; McDonald's posts bouncers, Kentucky Fried Chicken has an express line for parole violators and sex offenders.

Lunch is fast, faddish food that can be eaten while walking:

Frozen yogurt = the hot fad of 1979, now dated.

Hot dogs = politically incorrect; not to be eaten in mixed company.

Ham-filled croissants = basically a hot dog, but since it's French, it's currently la rave.

Chipwich (ice cream sandwiched between chocolate chip cookies) = the hit of 1981, now losing its edge.

Oversize cookies in a wax bag = At a dollar a cookie, they threaten to take over the city.

Pizza = old reliable. Watch for dripping grease!

Gyros = prison meat roasted on a greasy spit for twelve years, stuffed into a pouch of pita-shaped wet cardboard. Delicious.

How to Find an Affordable Dinner

Why cook when you can order in? Why order in when you can eat out? Some nights it seems like the whole city is on shore leave. The problem for most of us is how to afford it.

Keep these rules in your pocket, close to your wallet:

  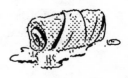

Food is politics. When you've got six bucks burning a hole in your pocket, think ethnic—but not sitcom ethnic. Turn to the Third World, the oppressed, the dispossessed. Read the *New York Times* "Week in Review" with an eye for revolutions and coups. The less assimilated a culture and cuisine, the lower the prices.

Forget about hanging ferns. Ferns do not make food taste good. Smoked glass and dim lights will never jazz up phony veal.

Location means nothing once you're inside. What a restaurant spends on rent, it cannot spend on food.

Armed with this knowledge, and some Maalox, take to the melting pot.

Little Ukraine (Second Avenue, Sixth to Ninth streets)

Little Poland (First Avenue, First to Twelfth streets)

Both strips serve good, hearty, stick-to-your-ribs fare. The perfect meal to tide you over before an outward-bound trek through the snow-covered Andes.

Little India (Sixth Street between First and Second avenues)

Piped-in Ravi music, mismatched dishware, and better service than you'll get in an operating room.

Cuban/Chinese (Comidas Chinas y Criollas) (Scattered on Eighth and Ninth avenues, and again north of Eighty-sixth Street on Broadway and Amsterdam)

When Castro took Cuba, Chinese merchants took a powder. Some opened restaurants with menus long enough to frustrate Evelyn Wood. Complete selection of Latin dishes, and the last stand for Cantonese food in the big city. Waiters speak Chinese, Spanish, English, some Creole; whatever *you* speak, they will resent it.

Little Szechuan/Little Hunan (Broadway, Ninetieth to One Hundredth streets)

Assimilating quickly, prices still reasonable. Beg for red peppers or they'll hold back.

Little Lebanon (Atlantic Avenue between Hicks and Clinton streets, Brooklyn)

Middle East meets Brooklyn: "Yo, lemme getta baba ganoush on rye with mayo, to go."

Little Odessa (Brighton Beach Avenue, between Brighton First and Brighton Seventh streets, Brooklyn)

Garlic and vodka. You'll never get sick again. Listen to the old immigrants complain about the new ones.

How to Be Humiliated at an Unaffordable Meal

New York is filled with elegant restaurants all predicated on de Sade's concept of pleasure through humiliation. Your maître d'—once a goatherd in Sardinia—greets you at the door and cringes as you enter. Your best clothes barely eke by the restaurant's vague code of "appropriate attire."

Although you might think of the maître d' as the man who seats you, in New York it's his job *not* to seat you. Flow with it.

Try slipping him a gratuity. He will respond by mortifying

Games New Yorkers Play

Health Code Sweepstakes

New Yorkers have little to look forward to in their lives. On Sundays, though, the papers publish the Health Department's weekly list of food establishments in violation of the city's health code. While everyone shares the misery of New York traffic and grime, the list provides a rare chance to feel special, to shed anonymity. It's like knowing someone who has become famous. New Yorkers scrutinize each listing in the desperate hope that their own hangout has that special notoriety:

Has the corner coffee shop *violated the code*?

Has the spartan sushi parlor *corrected last week's violations*?

Has the gyro/souvlaki/agar stand been *forced to close*?

The list is egalitarian—chop suey joints fester alongside high-tech nouvelle-cuisine kitchens; donut shops rub filth-encrusted elbows with corporate dining rooms.

If your nomination missed this week, don't despair. The Health Department says New York, which once had a light for every broken heart on Broadway, now has "a rat for every man, woman, and child in the city."

you for such a crass gesture, then he'll suavely palm the bill, and finally he'll resume ignoring you.

After two drinks at the bar, and three bowls of fish-shaped crackerettes, the maître d' will motion to you.

Yes! he is finally seating you . . . at that intimate table right off the men's room. He has done his job. You and the rest of the city will keep coming to his restaurant, desperate for one inkling of respect.

How to Judge a Restaurant

New York is ethnic wonderland. No one speaks English. In some neighborhoods it's easier to buy *wor bar* and *mofongo* than a burger. No matter how "up" you are on geopolitics, there's always a new form of Third World heartburn ready to assault you. Restaurant reviews can point you in the right direction, but the only reliable way to judge a restaurant is by studying the celebrity photos in the window.

It used to be easy: Bob Hope ate at bland Cantonese restaurants; Frankie, "Ol' Blue Eyes," hit all the Little Italy squid joints. When you saw their head shots in the window, you knew what was on the burners. Nowadays you have to be a regular maven to match the celebrities with their cuisine:

1. Window Photo: Alan Alda (posing in kitchen with illegal aliens).
Restaurant: Politically correct, semihot and spicy Szechuan.
2. Window Photo: Telly Savalas (autographed, "Who loves ya food, baby?").
Restaurant: Assimilated coffee shops with Greek owners. Waiters wear black pants, white shirts, work nineteen hours a day. You may be taking your life in your

hands by ordering anything other than eggs or a burger. Ixnay on the scallops.

3. Window Photo: Meryl Streep.

Restaurant: Nouvelle cuisine. High prices, Catalina decor, and a slightly boring but clean meal. Do not eat with your fingers here.

4. Window Photos: John Kennedy, Robert Kennedy, Charo.

Restaurant: Generally good Cuban food. Stray from ordering the Bay of Pigs stew.

5. Window Photo: Lindsay "Bionic Woman" Wagner.

Restaurant: Midtown working-class. Try the dietetic plates: meatball heroes, sausage-and-pepper omelets on kaiser roll.

6. Window Photo: Sylvester "Rocky" Stallone (poster, wearing boxing trunks; misspelled signature).

Restaurant: Local pizza parlors. Good *slices;* try to affect a Brooklyn accent: "Yo, lemme getta slice." Or simply: "Yo. Slice." Do *not* order a *piece* of pizza. Remember to fold your slice in half lengthwise after loading it up with garlic salt, onion salt, pepper flakes, and oregano. Practice eating your folded slice and walking at the same time. Now you're cool. Extra points for dripping the oil onto the sidewalk rather than your shirt.

7. Window Photo: Al Pacino (stock head shot).

Restaurant: Pizza parlors in up-scale neighborhoods. Often lukewarm and re-re-reheated. Acceptable here to eat slices with a plastic knife and fork.

8. Window Photos: Henny Youngman; Joey Adams; former Mayor Abe Beame (posing with restaurant manager, who stoops to shield height differential).

Restaurant: Midtown deli. How does eight bucks for a pastrami sandwich strike you? Originators of the I Hate New York Diet.

BASIC DIALOGUE: NEW YORK WAITER-SPEAK AND TRANSLATION

WAITER-SPEAK	TRANSLATION
I don't mean to rush you.	Get out!
Are you finished yet, sir?	Do you have an eating disability?
There's a cover here.	You must pay rent for this table.
I'll be right with you.	You don't have a prayer of being served.
Do you know about to-night's special?	You're about to pay fifty-seven dollars for month-old haddock.
Sorry, not my station.	Your mama's calling you.
What else?	There's a minimum here.
There's a minimum here.	Kiss your wallet good-bye.

How to Enjoy New York Night Life

There's so much to do in New York! Imagine living near the blazing lights of Broadway. Most New Yorkers pay so much rent to be near those blazing lights, they have no money left over for going out on the town.

Most New Yorkers stay home and watch TV. Sometimes they bowl or wait on line to see a movie.

Singles' Bars—Saturday Night Is the Loneliest Night of the Week

No one is ever lonely in New York.

Ever.

Just as, at the first sign of infection, you might go to a hospital, in New York, at the first sign of loneliness, you can go to a singles' bar.

In fact you can pick someone up in a singles' bar, then pick up an infection, and finally go back to that hospital referred to in the above metaphor.

You're probably saying, "I don't know, singles' bars, metaphors—they're not for me."

Probably you're right. But short of taking social work classes at the New School, there are no alternatives to meeting people in Fun City.

How to Present Yourself in a Singles' Bar

1. Never admit you're depressed.

2. Never mention herpes.

3. Stop your conversation when "New York, New York" comes on the jukebox. Sing along real loud, especially on the overwrought ostinatos. Punch the air when Frankie gets to the part about making it in the city that never sleeps.

4. *Never, ever* admit to being from Queens, Brooklyn, New Jersey, the Bronx, or Missouri. Always say you are from Manhattan. All non-Manhattanites are known as "River Rats," or "B and T's" (for Bridge and Tunnel), or "Strictly BBQ" (Bronx, Brooklyn, Queens). The terms are always derogatory. Sophisticates assume you chew gum while eating Chinese food.

How to Make a Pickup

If you're a guy,   1) Decide which gal you want to take home.

2) Be yourself.

3) Act natural.

4) Remember to flash a twelve-inch-thick wad of hundreds, a vial of coke, and a Pez dispenser jammed with 'Ludes.

If you're a gal,

1) Decide which guy you want to go home with.

2) Since every guy at the bar will ply you with disabling drugs, *choose early in the evening*.

3) Avoid men who talk excessively about Jodie Foster or wear synthetics.

4) Never take a shower in a stranger's apartment.

Where to Go

The Upper East Side: —still the Meat Rack, although the Great Herpes Panic of 1982 has cut down the crowds. Second Avenue is ethnic and déclassé. Opening line: "What are you, in banking or in retail?"

Third Avenue is gin-and-tonic land; try, "Whoo, boy, the market took a tumble today."

On First Avenue it's hospital orderlies who try to pick up single-gals-looking-for-doctors: "Yo, lemme get two cc's of Scotch in a club soda solution."

SoHo: —less overtly sexual. The trick here is to talk postneopostism for a few minutes, and *then* offer the cocaine.

Midtown: —action starts early at select hotels and businessman bars. Well-dressed women fill the bar area; it looks like a freshly stocked lake. "Any woman at the bar—a hundred fifty bucks," the maître d' will inform you.

Alternative to the Singles' Bar Scene

Adult education is a fast-growing fad in New York. It makes no difference what course you sign up for, as long as the class has a good male/female ratio.

Every week people pair up and drop out. If you haven't connected by the fifth week, bring a yellow pad to the class and experiment with taking notes.

Comedy in New York

"Hey, New York, comedy center U.S.A. How 'bout those comedy clubs, nice places . . . especially if you're a sardine . . . no, but seriously, these places have a golden history . . . the only other place you'll find guys this funny is at the post office. . . . What has two legs, grew up in a tough neighborhood, and thinks toilet and Quaaludes are the two funniest words in the English language? . . . Give up? I don't know, either, but he's always on stage at New York's famed comedy clubs."

Don't be surprised if some of the jokes sound familiar. Also, don't sit in the front row if you want to maintain a low profile: "Is that your wife with you, sir, or are you here on a convention?"

Games New Yorkers Play

Celebrity Name-Dropping

New Yorkers do not know how to enjoy hobbies, sports, family, or quiet nights alone. In order to maintain a little self-respect, they try to make others believe life in New York is glamorous. They drop names as fast as chunks of concrete dropping off the West Side Highway:

Good: I saw Meryl Streep in SoHo.

Better: I saw Meryl Streep and Robert De Niro talking to Kurt Vonnegut and Marty Scorsese at that new SoHo café.

Clichéd: I saw Woody Allen on Fifth Avenue with his collar up.

Bad: I saw Woody Allen on Fifth Avenue . . . actually, I saw Tony Roberts walking with somebody who I think was . . .

Boring: I saw Jill Clayburgh on the Upper West Side shopping at Zabar's.

Cabbies only: I just had Jackie O in my cab.

Rare and good: I saw Katharine Hepburn biking on the East Side.

Excellent: I saw Stevie Wonder and Paul McCartney jamming with some kids in Washington Square Park, it was incredible. . . .

Bad bluff: I saw Princess Di at my Laundromat doing a load of permanent press.

NEIGHBORHOODS

New York is a country unto itself. It has nothing in common with the rest of America. There are no shopping malls, no marching bands, no gawky teen-agers mowing lawns.

Graffiti proclaim: U.S. OUT OF NEW YORK NOW!

If New York is a country unto itself, the neighborhoods are best thought of as little fiefdoms. There is no central government in this city (you may test this by trying to phone any city agency).

New Yorkers know only their own neighborhoods, their turf. They'll walk two miles to avoid taking a new, unfamiliar subway line. They get nervous when they leave their zip code.

Like the large insane asylum it is, each ward has its own psychotic characteristics, its own asocial personality traits. Come, make the rounds. . . .

Wall Street

The center of white-collar crime in America. A million guys in pinstripes singing "Gimme Tax Shelter, Gimme Tax Shelter." The definition of a Wall Street iconoclast is an executive who wears a *belted* Brooks Brothers raincoat.

If you glue a ten-dollar bill to the sidewalk here, no one will stoop to pick it up. If, instead, you glue a blank restaurant receipt, you will stop traffic.

It's corporate largesse on a stick: large, sculpture-laden outdoor plazas, squash courts in the sky, taxis on radio call

CAN YOU SPOT THE ANARCHIST?

only. Even the Good Humor man gives two receipts: one for the company expense account, the other for tax fraud.

Clinton

See "Chelsea."

Greenwich Village

A neighborhood composed primarily of shoe stores, Greek gyro/souvlaki stands, and head shops. The deviant leather-goods shops are probably not a good place to buy Dad's Father's Day wallet.

Points of Interest:

Bohemia: Some haunts remain from this romantic district, but you do have to know where to look (see chart).

Washington Square Park: An antiamusement park crammed with bad, burnt-out rock musicians; bad drugs at unreasonable prices; and the constant threat of collision and demolition by brakeless bikers, Ripple-filled roller skaters, violent Frisbee criminals, New York University law students, and sex-starved Third World soccer players.

Twice-a-year home to the Washington Square Art Show (Memorial Day Weekend and Labor Day Weekend): This hideous art show, once limited to a few square blocks, has metastasized over much of the Village. Better to stare at the sun in total eclipse than to look at these oil-on-velvet renderings of harbors at sunset.

Times Square

A unique symbiotic partnership between city, business, and crime. The city leases Times Square for commuters during rush hours and for theatergoers in the few minutes before curtains rise on Broadway. At all other times, a consortium of dealers, pimps, and gunmen exercise firm control.

Point of Interest:

The Broadway Pickpocket Training School: Young would-be thieves from all over the world compete to enter this prestigious academy. Graduates are assured lifetime employment in many fields: fencing hot goods, three-card monte, fake-drug dealing, and, of course, pickpocketing. Students study day and night in stores, restaurants, and on the street. Many relax and unwind at the Times Square subway stations as well. The final exam is held once a year, on New Year's Eve. (Note: Three-card monte is a shell game in which pedestrians bet on which of three face-down cards is a red ace. The odds are with the house here because most often none of the face-down cards is a red ace.)

	BOHEMIAN ERA 1900–1956	CONDOMINIUM ERA 1978 TO DATE
HOUSING	Small, cold-water garret in a dilapidated five-story walk-up. Rent of eighteen dollars a month paid to crazy Lithuanian artist/landlord who cooked soup for you when you were sick. Artist later went mad and founded abstract expressionism.	Same apartment has now been divided into six closet-size pied-à-terres, co-op priced at $150,000 apiece, plus monthly maintenance. Building managed by Swiss-based international conglomerate. Still no hot water.
CAFÉ DISCUSSION TOPICS	Free love, class struggle, jazz, poetry. All debates fueled by double espressos (to facilitate fast-paced flow of ideas and creativity).	Insider prices on co-ops, market research, what it means if you wear your key chain on left side of hip, cable TV, *Gentlemen's Quarterly*. All diluted by decaffeinated cappuccinos, Perrier, Soave Bolla/club soda spritzers.
MUSIC	Charlie Parker, Krzysztof Penderecki, Pete Seeger.	Styx, Christopher Cross, Peter Allen. All forms of bad white popular music, especially show tunes.
MACDOUGAL STREET	Bohemia Central. John "Warren Beatty" Reed, Margaret "The Pill" Sanger, and more hanging out at the Liberal Club; discuss remaking society. Down the block Edna St. Vincent Millay acting in Eugene O'Neill's playhouse.	Gum-chewing, reefer-addicted juvenile delinquents from Jersey hang out at pizzeria on corner, play video games. Rest of the block is gyro/souvlaki/roach capital of Western world.

How to Find a Bathroom

In this town, if you carry a loaded bladder, you're an outlaw.

Restaurants shun you, lock you out, or shame you.

The City ignores you.

Businesses turn their backs on your needs.

There are strategies:

Act Cool

If you need to use a bathroom, *act as if you belong*. At the Pierre Hotel, pretend you're a disgraced president or a South American general.

At NYU Drama School, talk Method.

Think Big

Remember that millions of people work, shop, eat, and get depressed in Manhattan. Every day. Logically they must excrete here as well.

The following institutions would rather not serve you, but there is little they can do to stop you, especially if you *act cool*:

Hotels: Highest rank in the pantheon of pissoirs. Look for the big hotels with conferences and convention rooms (called, oddly, "function rooms"). These places don't dare stop you. Glide right up to the mezzanine level.

Office buildings: Less reliable. There is a way to crack these gleaming tax-avoiding towers of concrete and steel. From across the street look for the cafeteria floor, identifiable by its banks of unpartitioned lighting. Cafeterias don't have receptionists. Bermudas and backpacks will get you bounced pronto.

Atriums: Glass-enclosed, fern-choked public spaces built in exchange for zoning code exemptions. Use their awkwardly located restrooms. You've paid for them.

Restaurants: Located at foot of greasy staircase; floors look like subway cars after a sleet storm. Always use the facilities just before you leave. File for reference those bathrooms not guarded by management thugs.

Department stores: Should be ashamed. Millions for renovation and glitzy supergraphics, not a penny for tissue. Boycott their yogurt shops.

Subway bathrooms: Unsafe at any speed. Charlie Manson wouldn't lift a leg here.

Midtown

While midtown is headquarters for virtually every major international oligopoly and cartel, nothing has been produced here, that is to say manufactured, since 1947. It is a white-collar universe. The only calluses here are on the fingers of three-card-monte dealers.

"Air rights" are traded like playing cards and have been extended to cover private parks, churches, phone booths, and exceptionally short, slow-moving people.

By the end of the decade, if all goes according to plan, midtown will be completely sheltered from the natural world.

Business and city government are working hand in pocket for a darker tomorrow.

Alphabetland/"Loisaida"
(Avenues A through D)

The area used to be an outback, a goiter on Manhattan's lean neck. Isolated, without even a subway station, the neighborhood became New York's premier free-trade zone for narcotics—no small accomplishment. Recently, because a few of its buildings were still standing, the neighborhood became "hot" to the realtors.

For now an uneasy truce prevails between poor families, "young would-bes" fleeing surreal rents, and career criminals. In general, your apartment won't get robbed while you're inside it. If you go out for lunch, however, you might return to learn that junkies have cleaned out your place and even stolen your view.

Brooklyn

Lots of guys named Vinnie.

Columbus Avenue/Lincoln Center

The neighborhood is hot now. White hot. In little over five years, Columbus Avenue has gone from Bodega Row to *the* strip; *the* playground for the reformed children of the sixties. Instead of marching, they now don unstructured jackets and promenade; where once was heard the chant of ''Peace now!'' they fill cafés with orders of ''Quiche now, quiche now.''

Clothing: Window displays are bizarre and spartan. Mannequins are bald and posed in unnatural positions. Inside find two-hundred-dollar sweaters and fifty-dollar cummerbunds. One size clips all. Look for: The Evil Blouse and Melanzana Non Troppo (lit., Eggplant, not too much).

Ice cream parlors: Companies assume odd, vowel-deranged names to affect a Scandinavian image. You need financing for a malted. Flavors: Broccoli-quiche chip, Hunan–beef-flavored yogurt.

Food marts: Moe's Big City Deli is gone, replaced by gourmet shops like Le Pluperfect Pasta, Cry the Beloved Country Pâté, and L'Avuncular Avocado.

Restaurants: Serve up clean cuisine—brook sushi, melon toast; the cutting edge of the trendy and tasteless. If you dip your bread in gravy, they'll run you up on a morals charge.

Shoe Repair, Laundry, Hardware, and other Basics: Sorry.

Points of Interest:

Lincoln Center: Your petro-dollars at work
Mormon Center: (2 Lincoln Square—Church of Jesus
Christ of the Latter Day Saints, New York Visitors Center.)
They give free tours daily here.

Staten Island

Lots of guys with crew cuts.

Point of Interest:

The Staten Island Ferry: Each year, thousands of tourists
and lovers take the famous ferry to Staten Island. Upon arrival they immediately grab the next ferry back to Manhattan. No one has ever gotten off the boat.

Traveler's Advisory

Friendly New Yorkers
As a tourist in New York, you may occasionally
find yourself lost or confused. Relax. The New
Yorker is far more confused than you'll ever be.
Often the New Yorker will guide you completely
the wrong way; his warped sense of courtesy pre-

vents him from admitting he has never learned north from south. If a pedestrian is *real friendly* to you, just like people back home, get the hell out! The guy probably sells people like you into white slavery.

More common is the fabled New York Sarcastic-Constructive Mode of Response. Another necessary defense mechanism, one you should not take personally:

TOURIST	NEW YORK S.-C. MODE
Excuse me, do you have the time?	What am I, Big Ben?
Do you know if the F train stops at Fiftieth Street?	Lady, do I look like an information booth?
I'd like to get to Central Park.	Nobody's stopping you.
Is this the ticket holders' line?	No. All these people are standing here by coincidence.
Is it supposed to rain today?	What am I, nature boy?
Boy! Did you know you almost ran over that old lady?	What are you, her mother?

East Village

A melting pot, now being cooled off by gentrification. Still home to Ukrainians, Indians, Poles, hippies, and many other bad dressers. One walk down Second Avenue and you'll learn how to say "Spare change?" in seven different languages.

If you stop to chat, you'll also learn that "OPEC is a
wish conspiracy," and "Tricia Nixon sleeps with
rses." Don't stop to chat.

Finally, watch for black-clothed, androgynous anorectic
nks in varying stages of decay; you'll recognize them by
eir pale skin and beach-size trust funds.

Facts About Little Italy (pronounced "Li'el I'aly"):

- There are now more Chinese than Italians in Little Italy.
- Little Italy is all side streets. The side streets are filled
with cigar stores that don't sell cigars, candy stores
with no candy, and newspaper stores with no newspapers. Don't ask why.
- There are three remaining Italian bars. Their jukeboxes
play only "New York, New York," by the Chairman
of the Board ("Ol' Blue Eyes"), "Al-Di-La" by either
Enzo Stuarti or Ray Charles, and "Help Me, Rhonda."
- A cappuccino and cannoli at an outdoor café cost more
than dinner for six at a Chinese restaurant down the
block. Don't ask why.
- Favorite names: Richie, Joey, Angie. Most people also
respond to "Hey, yo!" or "Whadayou? Stupid or
something?"
- Old ladies in this neighborhood are surgically attached
to their windowsills.
- There are more big American cars in this neighborhood than in the rest of the city put together. If you
drive an economy car, you are a *faggot*.
- Favorite expression: "Do the right thing, Richie, do
the right thing." (Delivered with arm around shoulder
of addressee.)

	UPPER WEST SIDE	UPPER EAST SIDE
HISTORY	While the U.S. was sending Nixon to the White House, the Upper West Side was electing Bella Abzug as their congressperson.	Once called the silk-stocking district; presumably it is now called the silk pantyhose district, or L'Eggs district.
PROFILE	Home to musicians, writers, and other losers. Feiffer's people. Even after getting mugged, likely to remain liberal. Recently, lawyers and junior execs have been spotted moving their chrome lamps and Haitian cotton sofas in.	Old money—fortunes were not made in retailing or dentistry. The streets are clean; blond, blue-eyed babies get wheeled around by black mothers; doormen speak English and read **The Wall Street Journal.** Law-and-order disciples who've never been mugged.
FAVORITE PHRASES	"I'm having an anxiety attack." "We're gonna go on rent strike and make our scumbag landlord beg . . ."	"As long as you don't have to dip into capital."

"Jeanie, didn't Daddy tell you not to be hyper with Mommy?"

FOOD

Under the Szechuan West Redevelopment Plan for the Upper West Side, Broadway is becoming a one-mile-long Chinese restaurant.

Well-run coffee shops. Upper East Siders shun sushi and squid; they are capitalists, and capitalists eat red meat. Buy a burger here and watch blue-haired aspic-eaters undertip.

POINTS OF INTEREST

Columbia University: watch bearded guys in elbow-patched sweaters discuss Sino-Soviet relations in the 1950s.

Yorkville: the city's old Germantown. Look for signs like YORKVILLE TOWERS and LITTLE GERMANY CROISSANTERIE. Fine examples of the New York entrepreneurial tradition of naming new ventures after the neighborhood they helped to obliterate.

Queens

Lots of cemeteries and a dead baseball team.

Points of Interest:
Chinatown

The streets are paved with fish, the sidewalks lined with sweatshops. Many dialects spoken here, but cash is the common tongue. The definition of a Chinatown pervert is a man who prefers women to money.

Chelsea

See "Clinton."

Murray Hill

See "Columbus, Ohio."

IF YOU MUST
LIVE IN NEW YORK

Think! Do you really want to go through with this? It is never too late to buy a few postcards and go back home. If you are coming to New York, you will want especially to cut and save the following chapter; keep it with you, in a secure place. Unfortunately, if you are coming to New York, you will not have a secure place.

The New York Factors

If you are moving to New York you should at all times be aware of what urban sociologists have dubbed "The New York Factors":

1) Nothing runs smoothly in New York—if a trip should take half an hour, allow at least three hours and forty-five minutes.

2) Everything costs more in New York . . . a lot
more. Wear hockable clothing.

Now let's see how these factors work on a day-to-day level.

Marketing Chores

Daily marketing is complicated by the fact that in New
York it is against the law for small shops to be owned by
English-speaking people.

If you're buying vegetables, bring your Korean phrase
book along. Learn the correct tones for such phrases as:

> Is this ripe?
> Do you have fava beans?
> Why are these cantaloupes emitting steam?

At hardware stores and stationery shops, you'll need to
pantomime your needs; simple requests, like "Molly bolts"
and "Ko-Rec-Type," might be understood. Marcel Marceau
couldn't purchase latex wall-covering here. Stock up when
out of town.

At pharmacies and hospitals, wait until you've reached
the later, more symptomatic stages of a particular disease.
Try to avoid psychological and internal problems.

Post Office

The postal service in New York City is modeled on the Italian civil service. It is a void: people and letters disappear
inside its slaty walls never to be seen again.

Most New Yorkers plan their weekends around trips to
the post office—allow four hours to buy stamps; allow
eleven weeks to mail a package from one part of the city to
another.

Banks

See "Post Office."

Also, note: Not even cash can impress the city's banks. Open a checking account with it, and you'll still be asked to wait thirty days for it to clear.

To get change for a ten, you must produce identification: major credit cards, your high school yearbook, and the doctor who brought you into this world.

Try to avoid these banks:

> The New York Bank for Waiting
> Aggravation Handover
> Manhattan Savings and Red Line

Also, as a matter of sound fiscal policy, local banks cannot issue loans to New Yorkers or New York businesses. You understand.

Laundromats

Owned and managed by Luddites. The washers and dryers are frustrated incinerators; they take no prisoners.

The Laundromats themselves provide shelter to New York's roustabouts. Transvestites, cadavers, and night stalkers all sleep here during the day. Generally they strip down to their abused bodies and wash everything they own all at once. Laundromats are the world's largest tetanus breeding grounds. Think before you sit.

The Great Outdoors

Escape from New York can be difficult. On weekends it can be impossible. Fortunately, throughout the city's boroughs are miles and miles of public beach. Some may prefer the

white sand beaches of the Caribbean, or the rocky shore of
the Riviera, but New Yorkers swear by the crushed-glass-
and-cigarette sand of Orchard Beach and the Brooklyn
coast. Get psyched up by taking the eighty-minute subway
ride to these locations. Don't you love that smell?

Health Clubs

While many Americans think of their bodies as temples, the
New Yorker is apt to think of his body as a lobby.

The Great Outdoors has been moved indoors. For about
eight hundred dollars a year, New Yorkers can wait on line
to bench-press and knee-jerk, or perhaps to swim in the jar-
sized pool. Space is always at a premium in New York, and
most of these places have to condense the locker rooms in
order to wedge in the more important quiche-and-salad bar.

Supermarkets

In American suburbs, supermarkets are clean, well stocked,
and well managed. Clerks are courteous and shoppers po-
lite. In New York, the shopping carts have been vandalized,
the aisles have potholes, and the counters are wiped down
with Pepsi.

Even grocery stores here serve as unofficial halfway
houses. Staff members tend to get a little jaded as a result.

How to Rent an Apartment

New York is a city of over seven million people and
forty-three affordable apartments. None of these are vacant
right now. When you move to New York you might find
yourself on a friend's couch for a few weeks. Eventually
you will join the Sublet-of-the-Month Club; you will become an urban nomad. Do not despair. This guide will
help.

How Bad Is the Market?

It's never been worse. The entire city has been playing musical chairs, and the music has finally stopped. Wherever you are at that moment is where you may live the rest of your life. All over the city people are frozen in apartments, marriages, and relationships they do not like; they dare not move.

> **She:** My grandmother just died.
> **He:** What kind of apartment did she have?
> **She:** She was a lovely woman.
> **He:** Wasn't it a prewar one-bedroom?

Aren't There Any Shortcuts?

The most favored technique is bribery; bribery on a scale unseen since Naples at the end of World War Two. Superin-

BASIC DIALOGUE
AT THE SUPERMARKET DELI COUNTER

Old lady

Give me a quarter pound, and slice it thin!

Deli man

Is this thin enough? (displays boiled ham)

Old lady

I said **thin**, not **thick**! Slice it thin!

Deli man

Lady, this is thin.

Old lady

That's not thin. You never slice it thin!

Deli man (to coworker)

Oh-oh, here she goes.

Old lady

Don't be rude. Slice it thin! I live alone. Where's your boss. You are so rude. . . . They should fire you.

Deli man

Lady, you want it thin, I give it to you thin. What do you think—

Old lady

They should throw you in jail. . . .

Deli man

Lady, you want to fire me. You want to fire me? I'm quitting this job. I'm getting out of here. You know why? Because of people like you. It's people like you that drive me crazy. All you can do is bitch. . . . I hope you have a heart attack and die. . . . I hope you have a heart attack and die right here. Die, lady . . . but your kind never dies.

Games New Yorkers Play

"Can You Top This?"

This is a game New Yorkers love to play, usually at dinner parties. The object of the game is to see who can come up with the most horrifying personal experience in a given topic area. The topic is always chosen from among the numerous degrading aspects of life in New York: apartment hunting, subway horror, neighborhood terror.

Usually someone starts things off by relating a recent dehumanizing experience; for example: "I had to wait on line for twenty minutes to buy a subway token today. Only one guy was selling tokens and the other four sat inside the booth reading *Hustler* magazine and laughing about how long the line was!"

Once this *opening gambit* is thrown, the conversation whips around the table at a dizzying pace. No one is allowed to complete a story, regardless of how harrowing it may seem. Instead he must be cut off abruptly with *"That's nothing, I was . . ."* Example: "That's nothing, I was on the subway the other day, and this crazy guy was spitting blood and screaming, 'The Trilateral Commission knows that peanuts cause cancer, but they won't tell the people.' Well, he finally gets off at Fifty-ninth Street and everyone starts to laugh, only another bum gets on at the *same* stop, and takes the *same* seat, and he starts spitting blood and shouting, 'Disney stole Porky Pig from me. I was in the army and Disney stole . . .' "

The game usually ends when everyone has played at least twice and people aren't even bothering to interrupt each other. By this time "The train was incredible. I kept going from car to car and there was always a guy vomiting in the corner, four kids breaking windows, and another guy vomiting in the corner at the other end . . . it was like Calcutta or something."

When the quiche, salad Niçoise, and Soave Bolla arrive at the table, the game is officially over.

---

tendents get *key money,* friends get *finder's fees,* tenants signing an apartment over to you get *fixture fees* (figure roughly one thousand dollars per shelf they've installed). Brokers and agents get a third of your gross salary for the term of the lease, plus twenty years.

To avoid this path, be cagey. Scan the obituary columns for violent, sudden deaths. Read the *Post* for particularly gruesome murders; mass murders provide a better choice of neighborhoods. Where there's a corpse, there's liable to be an empty apartment!

Befriend frail, old people. Encourage them to lead more active lives. Try something like "Mom, Dad . . . I think you two should take up hang-gliding." (Many a subletting New Yorker is grappling with tough questions of ethics: Would you save a drowning man if you knew he had a two-bedroom rent-stabilized apartment?)

What's Next?

Soon you will be getting all kinds of housing leads. You may even start to look at actual apartments available for rent. Understand the language of the landlords:

Unspeakable luxury	A closet.
Light, airy apartment	Six-story walk-up. Bricks are loose.
Sunken living room	The key word here is *involuntarily.*
Exposed brick walls	You will get a better feel for how exposed the walls are when winter comes.
Quaint, cozy	A closet
No fee	Bribes accepted
Safe/Secure	Last tenant resting comfortably and is expected to recover after most recent break-in.

What Should I Do If I See an Apartment I Like?

This is very unlikely. You can't afford it anyway.

What Should I Do When a Landlord Insults Me by Showing Me a Subbasement Studio in a Terrible Neighborhood That He's Renting for $850 a Month?

Bribe him immediately! Do not let this one slip away. Offer to pay a thousand dollars; tell him you'll find roommates. Tell him he reminds you of your father.

What Happens If I Need the Super When Something Goes Wrong with my Apartment After I Move In?

In search of historic Jesus.

How Can I Bargain with Him?

Tell the landlord the apartment is wonderful, it's a dream. Tell him you realize what a favor he is doing by leasing it to you. Casually work into the conversation the possibility of his installing a working shower, a floor that meets the walls, a separate Roach Motel complex. Your landlord will smile and say "No problem." This means you are about to get hosed. It also means you'd better sign the lease before he begins to suspect you're a complainer. Grab the lease from his hand.

Now That I've Moved in, My Apartment Actually Seems to Have Shrunk?

A common phenomenon. Your apartment has indeed shrunk and will continue to do so for the term of the lease. Some New Yorkers find it helps them to refer to different corners of the same room as the dining room, living room, bedroom, and kitchen. It is therapeutic to shout at your roommate: "Honey, can you keep the kids quiet upstairs, I'm trying to get some work done down here."

New Yorkers on Vacation

1) New Yorkers on vacation always roll up their windows and lock their cars. Even in Oconomowoc, Wisconsin.
2) New Yorkers on vacation do not know what to do at a self-service gas station.

CAN YOU SPOT THE NEW YORKER?

3) New Yorkers on vacation always get sick. Home-cooke food and clean air send their overstimulated systems into shock.

4) New Yorkers on vacation do not know how to relax. They bring their briefcases to the beach; they wear suits to Disneyland.

5) New Yorkers on vacation can never admit that anything excites them.

6) New Yorkers on vacation will lapse into a deep cataton state if you try to show them your vegetable garden, carpe try workshop, sewing room, or knitting bag. They have no idea what you are talking about.

7) New Yorkers on vacation will spend hours looking for the coin slots on your basement washing machine.

8) New Yorkers on vacation go through *New York Times* and MSG withdrawal. (''Where's the *rest* of the newspaper?'')

9) New Yorkers on vacation love one-downmanship. No matter how tough or mean or dirty or corrupt something is the New Yorker has seen worse. You're strictly bush league.

> ''You think *this* is bad . . . you should see New York . . .''
> ''You call *this* rush hour traffic . . .''
> ''You think *this* is expensive . . .''

10) New Yorkers on vacation love one-upmanship. No ma ter where you take them, they will compare it, unfavorably to something in New York.

> ''You mean *this* is considered a good restaurant?''
> ''You mean *this* is downtown?''
> ''You mean this is the *Great* Wall?''

Traveler's Advisory

If You Must Stay with a New Yorker

1) Do not expect to be picked up at the airport—a trip to the airport takes two years off a New Yorker's life.

2) Do not expect your host to know where he lives in relation to highways or the outside world.

3) Do not bring a plant as a housewarming gift. New Yorkers do not like to be tied down to commitments.

4) Do not ask him where the rest of his apartment is.

5) Do not open closet doors in search of other rooms.

6) Do not expect a good, steady hot-water shower. If, while you are showering, someone somewhere on the Eastern Seaboard flushes a toilet, you will get scalded.

7) Do not attempt to light the oven. It probably doesn't work; if it does, there may be books in it.

8) Do not wake up at the crack of dawn and shout, "Gosh, it's grand to be alive."

ONE ROOM APT. WITH LIVE-IN OVEN.

I Hate Holidays in New York

All days in New York are bad, but these are the worst. The only things they have going for them are holiday parking regulations and the fact that each comes only once a year.

Winner

ST. PATRICK'S DAY, MARCH 17

This is the day, when, to honor the patron saint of the Irish, two hundred thousand kids from New Jersey and Long Island play hooky from school, come into the city, and vomit.

Avoid all streets and sidewalks and parks.

First Runner-Up

NEW YEAR'S EVE

1) If you decide to throw a party, no one will commit to coming in advance. The entire city hedges, holding out for a better invitation.

Woody Allen's party is hot; yours is not.

2) If you decide to go out on the town, you will guarantee yourself a new life of indigence:

—The local coffee shop is charging seventy-five dollars per person for a burger and beer.

—Taxis all drive with the off-duty light on. If you offer to pay their auto insurance for the decade, they'll deign to pick you up. They will not, however, drive you through midtown. "Too crowded, I no make money stuck in traffic. Ees crazy."

—Baby-sitters, including your mother-in-law, charge four times the normal rate.

3) Times Square. Join four hundred thousand drunken, dateless Methedrine freaks. They shoot off Molotov cocktails at midnight. Ees crazy.

Miss Congeniality

CHRISTMAS

New York kids do not fear Santa. Instead they go to department stores, sit on his lap, and taunt him. They tell him, "You'd better come across this year, fat man."

THE MANHATTAN S.A.T.
(Survival Aptitude Test)

Transportation Etiquette

1) You are reading a paper on the subway. A punk approaches you and says, "Boy, I like your shoes." You should:

    A) Try to find an article of his clothing to compliment, e.g.: "Thank you . . . say, your holster looks swell."

    B) Start twitching and then, as if in a rant, repeat: "It's only a movie, it's only a movie."

    C) Remove your shoes from your feet, and hand them up to the punk. Thank him. Ask him if he likes your socks.

2) You are riding in a bus. Twenty high school kids get on illegally through the back door. They are all smoking cigarettes and marijuana. One youth looks at you, then puts his cigarette out in your face. You should:

    A) Thank him for not smoking.

    B) Act natural.

    C) Apologize.

    D) Take the cigarette out of your face, and ask, "How do you find these low-tar cigarettes . . . tell the truth, don't you miss the flavor?"

IS THIS MAN TOO CRAZY TO SIT NEXT TO?

3) You are walking your date home late at night. A gang of teen-agers surround you and ask, "Got any spare change?" You should:

    A) Search your pockets and then say, "Sorry, I don't have anything smaller than a twenty."

    B) Shake your head, then say, "Gee, fresh out. Why don't you fellas wait here? I've got some change up-stairs."

    C) Press a button on your wristwatch and say, "Beam us up, Scottie, beam us up."

Geography

1) To a New Yorker, *Upstate* means:

    A) Nothing.

    B) Anything north of 125th Street.

    C) Canada.

2) To a New Yorker, the words *Idaho, Ohio,* and *Iowa* hold what meaning?

A) They are different pronunciations of the same state,
   the state that borders Kansas and Montana, on Lake
   Erie.
B) Three types of potato.
C) Two Indians and an oil company.
D) College towns.

True/False

Sparrows are baby pigeons.	T	F
Red light means stop.	T	F
You need a yellow vaccination card to get into Brooklyn.	T	F
All politicians are crooked.	T	F
It's not what you know, but who you know.	T	F
There's another train right behind this one.	T	F
It would be easier to carpet a coal mine than a New York subway station.	T	F
There are more psychiatrists on the corners of Eighty-sixth Street and Park Avenue than in thirty of the world's least developed countries put together.	T	F
I'll be right with you.	T	F
People from New York have seen it all.	T	F

Local Color

Which of the following would be an atypical expression for
a New Yorker?

A) Why make it yourself if someone else can make it
   for you?
B) If it doesn't work, throw it out.
C) No matter where I serve my guests, they always love
   my kitchen best.
D) Why own it if you can rent it?

Local Commerce

Which of the following signs would you be most likely to
see in a New York store?
- **A)** Checks gladly accepted.
- **B)** Good work makes beautiful things, and good work
  lasts.
- **C)** You break it, you buy it.
- **D)** Plenty of free parking.

Genius Test

Which of these people makes the most money in New
York?
- **A)** a real estate broker
- **B)** a pimp
- **C)** a therapist
- **D)** a locksmith

Essays

1) You witness a purse snatching. Like a good Samaritan,
you start running after the mugger. Much to your chagrin,
you find yourself catching up with him. What should you
do?

2) Write a short story about New York. Try to use as much
New York dialect as possible including, but certainly not
limited to, the following expressions:
- a) Gimme a break.
- b) So what could be new.
- c) Listen to me, Harry, you're not listening.
- d) Goddamn Mayor Lindsay.
- e) What's in it for me?
- f) Yo.
- g) Cop some reefer.

h) I can get it for you wholesale.
i) This week is *crazy*. Call me next week . . .
   we'll set something up.
j) Who wants to know?
k) Such a deal.